BAD GOVERNMENT
AND
SILLY LITERATURE

An Essay by

Carol Bly

Milkweed Editions

© 1986 by Carol Bly
All rights reserved. Published 1986
Printed in the United States of America

88 87   5 4 3 2

A THISTLE
Published by *Milkweed Editions*
an imprint of Milkweed Chronicle
Post Office Box 24303
Minneapolis, Minnesota 55424
Books may be ordered from the above address

This essay originally was published in Volume 7,
Number 1, the Winter 1986 issue of Milkweed Chronicle

ISBN: 0-915943-15-8

This publication is supported in part by grants provided by The First Bank System Foundation; the Jerome Foundation; Metropolitan Regional Arts Council from funds appropriated by the Minnesota State Legislature and with special assistance from the McKnight Foundation; by the United Arts Fund from the Arts Development Fund; the Pillsbury Company Foundation; and by the contributions of generous individuals.

1

If an American were to turn out a novel or story in the 1980s in which men and women characters consorted together without one mention of physical desire, we would wonder in reviews and at lunch why the author suppressed sexuality. Yet hundreds of novels and stories offer us American characters who live out their lives without any political and ethical anxiety. We ought to be calling it suppression, because we are as much political and moral creatures as we are sexual creatures.

Our cadre of serious writers—those who read fiction in the little magazines and *The New Yorker* and the *Pushcart* anthologies as a matter of course—have emotions about being citizens of the second cruellest government of our decade. I have assigned us second-place for cruelty although there are several small countries who are openly and equably much more ruthless than we: their victim-catchment area, however, is so much smaller than ours that they cannot generate as much grief as we can. My half-educated guess is that the first-place runner for cruelty, the Soviet Union, has lapped us several times. Nonetheless, the United States holds second place, and Americans who are educated, and who write stories, know it.

The two considerations of this essay are: a demonstration of how we can bring ethics-consciousness into our stories, so that we stop suppressing it, and second, how it is that our fiction has ignored ethical anxiety. For the sake of simplicity, let us limit ethics-consciousness to feelings of (1) shame for our nation and (2) fear for the planet itself.

We can eliminate the possibility that American fiction authors are so self-centered they have no shame for the United States or fear for the planet. Authors are as ethically grown up as members of other occupations. Most of them belong to and support the innumerable anti-war and anti-nuclear-use groups. They are perfectly aware that what our government does or fails to do has immense consequence.

It is therefore surprising that most of the characters in American fiction are fools. They are not meant to be fools: the protagonists and their friends and enemies go to college; they try to move from one-night stands into meaningful relationships. Their authors tend to be exhaustive on the subject. They try to have jobs that are more than just lucrative. Somehow, however, they have no political or ethical feelings. Well, then — we hypothesize — perhaps ethical grief is a form of stress and these characters don't feel stress. That doesn't wash. Never in any literature in any period of any nation's culture have so many fiction characters complained so much about stress as in our 1970s and 1980s books. They sigh. They act out. They explain to one another their psychological needs as relentlessly as a hospital patient explains to the morning-shift nurse just how awful the night has been. In fact, much of American fiction dialogue is Call Bell Pressing. Yet these characters conduct their joys and frets during unjust wars and terrible domestic poverty and never notice. They must step over the bodies of mental patients thrown into the streets, without noticing. There isn't an author in New York or St. Paul who doesn't notice the souplines, but our stories are about people who don't notice souplines. What all this means is not that our authors are deliberately presenting fools to the American reading public, but that they are following a convention of literature. The convention is to suppress ethical anxiety. Writers like John Knowles and William Golding burst past the convention: hundreds of writers don't even aim to escape it.

I will offer a cure. After describing the cure, I will present a reason for the disorder. But first of all, let me say there is no law that says we must take the cure at all. There is no law that says fictional characters must feel ethical malaise just because all of us in real life do. Ethical malaise in a character is not to be confused with the character's being a victim of injustice. Victims, goodness knows, have rightly made up the *dramatis personae* of plays and fiction through the ages. What we mean by ethical malaise being suppressed is that characters do not grieve over their government's cruelty. We can duck the whole question, if we like, in which case our literature will remain what it largely is now — rather too self-centered and capricious, with its plots full of private lovelife and financial considerations. If we leave it as it is, the other three main forces of public opinion today will shoulder ethical consciousness without us. These forces are the first-rate cartoonists like Gary Trudeau and the first-rate TV documentary makers, and the first-rate ethicists.

To run through them quickly: Trudeau all by himself is a gigantic source of ethical consciousness. He speaks to educated Americans of the grossness and falseness of specific federal-government policies. I would guess that in any given day thousands of Americans read *Doonesbury* and shout, "Oh yes! That's it—that's it, exactly!"

Second: it is possible that if "Sixty Minutes" devoted all its attention to United States government behaviors or large-corporation behaviors, that that one TV program could change the moral awareness of educated Americans. "Sixty Minutes," indeed, has added clout: unlike *Doonesbury*, it is loved by half-educated and uneducated people. People, schooled or not, who normally participate in no political or ethical thought are delighted by and somehow relieved by watching "Sixty Minutes."

Finally: the ethicists. It is important to understand a change in the field of Ethics. Ethics is no longer a thin, considered wail from university departments of Philosophy: it is now passing quickly, quickly, into developmental psychology, into education, into the other social sciences. It has lurched out of the Reasoning cage and into the exhilaration of *mental-image-making*. Ethicists are keen on simulation and situation study: they are much changed by *process*—in which each of us makes a mental image of ourselves in a given circumstance. They are in the forefront of intelligent thinking, too. The wide public of Ernest Becker and James MacGregor Burns and Lawrence Kohlberg and Carol Gilligan and Sissela Bok is made up not just of social scientists but of political activists and futurists and generalists of all kinds—and of writers.

This new brand of ethicist has a tremendous salient: it is that they believe an adult can change from being someone only technically proficient and technically awake into someone who is morally competent and ethically sensitive. A limited person in the private sector can become an energetic advocate in the public sector. These people talk a good deal about *leadership*, but when we writers look through their list of definitions of leadership, we find the same words we would use about *psychological health*. We are wise to ask, "Isn't leadership really just psychic health? All that being able to evaluate on your own, all that being able to make a mental image of the other fellow's situation, all that deliberately building on hope instead of resting on hopelessness, all that deliberate questioning of facile myth?" It is true that such a list defines both leadership and psychic health, but writers must also look at this: we are willing, in our twentieth-century conventionality, to show or tell about our characters' psychic health, but not about our characters' leadership. Psychology is now OK material for fiction. Apparently ethics-leadership is not yet approved.

I have said above that if American fiction goes on repressing ethical consciousness in its characters, then that ethical consciousness can likely be carried by cartoonists, television, and ethicists' lectures and books. Let us say there is a nice boy who is going to be the protagonist of our story. He goes to Middlesex or Andover and graduates from Penn or Yale. He is going to have 3.2 affairs in college, one later, a marriage, a divorce, another marriage more to his liking, some complicated and rewarding relationships with his children, some career difficulties when he is one of twenty-seven vice-presidents of his firm not to find room at the very top, a bout with a terminal disease in which he behaves first of all badly, then better, then quite valiantly, and then he dies. That is a workable regimen for an American novel hero. Bearing this man's life in mind, then, let us also ask what are two major ethical problems of our time? We are asking this because we believe the ethical component is part of human nature and because we are scared stiff of the United States government.

Let us say that two serious dilemmas are a) how can we make *groups* as well as individual people study their own behavior and learn to behave well instead of being irresponsible, and b) how do we get not just the tens of thousands of Americans now worried about American national behavior, but another few millions, at least, involved in the ethical-growth process?

2

A wonderful way to do it is to take the novel plot above and enfold into it the ethical cares and worries of the protagonist. Surely a nice boy from Andover and Yale has serious anxiety about his government, at least once! That malaise should be put into the book, so that other Andover and Yale boys will read it, and learn. America's upper-middle class, like any upper-middle-class in any country in any era, takes fiction characters as role models. Children know that Jo is good and Amy is bad, Meg is an acculturated female-role simpleton, and Beth is the wimp-of-all-the-ages. Horatio Hornblower is good and Iago is bad. Lord Jim was a pretty boy who was bad and he became good. And so on. No upper-middle-class person models himself on Dagwood or Archie Bunker because they are middle-middle-class and like East and West, the two classes do not meet.

Now let us suppose that inserted into a goodly number of novel plots, along with the 3.2 affairs in colleges, the marriages, the careers, the sicknesses and deaths, were scenes in which the CIA approached the Andover-and-Yale man and offered him a job and he turned it down—remembering Yuri Nosenke or simply knowing of any six of the CIA's various projects. If that incident went into the novel as naturally as one or two of the love affairs went into it, it would seem like reality—moral reality—just as the love affairs do. Tens of thousands of the kind of Americans who read Helprin and Tyler and O'Connor and Mansfield and Tolstoy would read about the man refusing to work for the CIA. Their own ethical malaise would be, to use the appalling but accurate social scientists' word for it, *validated*. That would be a change. Ethical malaise gets almost no validation in fiction as fiction is now.

For readers who somehow, even in 1986, have escaped the process called *validation*, let me explain that it means hearing that others—sane, not crazy others—have the same feelings you have and that those feelings are acceptable. Validation is psychological fact. The most recent incidents involving validation are the incest cases, where social workers and psychotherapists have desperately tried to assure children that it is OK to say what their uncle or father did, and that it is OK to feel bad that those bad relatives did those bad things. Unfortunately, when a person's feelings are not spoken and thus not validated, that person tends to dislike himself or herself for having the feelings. Women who were beaten used to feel guilty that they were beaten. When they hear sensible people talking about wife-beating, they realize that their suffering is validated. They recover their self-esteem.

The best case of validation is the story in Genesis 2:19. *And out of the ground the Lord God formed every beast of the field, and every fowl of the air; and brought them unto Adam to see what he would call them: and whatsoever Adam called every living creature, that was the name thereof.*

The Genesis author knew that we talk about what we honor as real, and, secondly, that when we name things that we partly love, we begin to love them better. God didn't give Adam permission to skip all that animal-naming: he told him to get it done. Consciousness-raising is largely naming. Only the ignorant say, "But just because I don't talk about it or mention it doesn't mean I don't love it and honor it!" Women were wise to insist on "inclusive language"—"him and her" instead of just "him," and "he and she" instead of just "he," and "humankind" instead of "mankind."

At the moment, there is almost no validation for upper-middle-class readers of American literature to take seriously the following acts:
    Refusing to work for especially spurious federal agencies
    Objecting to poisonous products of companies one works for when those companies also make wonderful products
    Exposing, even in conversation in drawing rooms over cocktails, crooked military arms procurement, and so forth

If a critical mass of our novels depicted characters who were nervous about those issues, the American upper-middle-class would be validated in its nervousness. The consciousness-raising would be nearly exquisite. We needn't do it particularly well. Tacky validation is better than suppression. I don't think John Updike writes very well about sex, but he writes about it, and nearly every literate American now knows that people enjoy shabby sex as well as lovely sex. We owe some of that insight to Updike.

3

American fiction writers won't do ethics consciousness-raising very skillfully at first. In a roomful of ethical thinkers, the writers tend to be the most childish. We tend to stay stuck at beating our breasts and crying, "My God, how can people do such godawful things anyway!" or offering all those remarks that begin with "I just can't understand how . . . . etc., etc!" Beginning moralists are always full of virtue. They feel ten times more sensitive than the people sitting next to them, and they want credit for all that sensitivity. Meanwhile, the social scientists and people who are good at management will be drumming fingers and saying, "Right! Now — how do we go about fixing this? What more data do we need, and what kind of staffing would be best here?" They begin to plan while the writers are still flaring their nostrils.

I think we can move from moral preening to sensible ethical-consciousness. It will involve some sacrifice. We will have to give over a good deal of the weird situations and grotesque private lives that we are fond of. People love Flannery O'Connor for her weird horrible people easily as much as they love her for her abiding theology. We will have to set aside some of the self-pitying conversations our characters have in favor of conversations in which the characters grieve about the government. It sounds dreary and hard, just as any New Year's resolution sounds, but we have Camus and Chekhov and ever Orwell out in front, an encouraging phalanx.

I expect American story-tellers will take on ethics-awareness; we still have freedom of press, we have more energy than writers living in totalitarian systems, and finally, our government, doing more terrible things every day, drives us to it. Once we start naming our ethical anxieties, we will honor them more: we will find an affection for this newly confessed passion — caring for the public weal.

4

At the beginning of this essay I promised a reason for our not having managed ethical anxiety in our fiction. The reason is not the only reason, but it is a powerful and complicated one. It is that most of our good books are written by people who grew up on fairy tales. Straightaway let me say that fairy-tale reading is wonderful in many ways, as Marie Louise von Franz and Bruno Bettelheim and now scores of other thinkers have told us. There are three results of fairy-tale reading that are not good.

What's a fairy tale? The king and queen forever control everything. Or worse, he controls everything and she goes along with it. Then the third child of some citizen or other spends an unpromising early childhood sleeping on the stove-back or sitting in the ashes. This child hears of the crisis, rouses himself or herself, gets help from the universe through a kindly relationship with plants or animals, and goes off to be very successful at the palace. Does that child then reform the government so it does not spend all its money at war, trampling over the neighboring fields, taking funds from the sick and the poor? The child may be a kindly totalitarian, but he or she does *not* change the status quo at all: the hero becomes a revisionist, not a reformer—and moves into the palace. Cinderella, we notice, did not call elections or make the prince design social programs to prevent child abuse by stepmothers: she got the prince to set up her sisters in luxury. She even found rich husbands for them—maintaining all the old institutions.

Children (future writers) reading those stories get no role modeling in changing the social order.

Determinists, who are always looking for a quick solution whereby one agrees that such-and-such an influence *always* factors on the situation in a certain way, will be glad to remain with the idea that if a young reader has no role models for changing the social order then the young reader will grow up into someone who will not change the social order. We have to remember that powerful influences do not always make the man or woman: reformers were brought up on fairy tales, too.

Let's look at the bad influence at closer range. Lack of good role models for social change is the obvious drawback to fairy-tale reading. To see a more subtle influence of fairy-tale reading, let us chart a person's development in *idealistic feelings*.

First stage: This is the stage in which children joyfully respond to fairy-tale reading. Anyone's first idealistic feelings, regardless of that person's actual physical age, take the form of private, alien quest. The parents of the I (or fairy-tale hero) are coarse, worldly, or outright and deliciously cruel. They act out every single collective shadow quality the most lightning-bright paranoid could think up. The siblings of the I are coarse, too: one's rivalry with them takes the form of seeing oneself as numinous and designated for finer things, whereas the siblings are in league with the cruel parents and are successful manipulators of the world, as well.

A crisis comes. (People who are ethically naive— beginners, that is—respond very well to crisis and not nearly so well to day-by-day, banal evil.) At the crisis, the young idealist in the fairy tale rouses from a half-sleep and dreaming state, is sneered at by parents and siblings, and leaves on a mission. On the way he or she makes a spiritual compact of some kind with *nature*, calling on some ancient force such as old women in the forest who know tricks, or by doing a kindness to some non-human creature or plant. The idealist typically shakes apples off an overloaded tree and gives holy water to a parched dog or returns a flounder to the sea. In return for these satisfying and good acts, the idealist gets eccentric spiritual equipment for the crisis task. Now the fact that the task as such is pure worldliness, such as getting a princess, setting up one's own family in wealth and prestige forever, doesn't bother the young idealist. We are looking at the prototype of the boy who will support his old mother, who will be kind to the servants, who will put the maid's two kids through college.

Second Stage: After one graduates from the boyish and girlish idealism above, one learns to sacrifice *stasis* for *flux*. One sees that the status quo is purely cruel to the powerless and the poor, and therefore we must change it. One leaves the comfort of daydreaming over what-ought-to-be. One leaves off imagining oneself cleanly a pilgrim. One joins others in order to *plan*.

Planning means something painful to the Stage One idealist: it means having to work with others. Ex-fairy-tale readers are of course prepared and even anxious to work with others in life, but what they hadn't really figured on was working with others in idealism. Idealism was their private activity.

A propos of this, I have always found it fascinating that the most brutal of cultures often cling to the most gorgeous and dramatic of mythologies: if one can keep the twilight of the Gods inside oneself like an old daydream, the treacheries of hammer-wielding bullies inside oneself, the onset of battle between the old earth forces and the new love forces — all safely inside oneself — where everyone told us it belonged anyway, then we can take our train to the Krupp works each day without confusion. All that government-making genius of the human brain can be expressed by cooperating with the factory powers that be or the bureaucracy powers that be — and not be connected to the mythology.

Trying to make social change is a sad business, in comparison to that cocooning of ideals apart from the group. One must move one's consciousness from the Art of the Ideal to the Art of the Possible. One can no longer hanker for emotional purity. Social technocrats are in this second stage: that is why they drum their fingers at the meeting where the writer is still crying out, "O how can people *treat* Salvadorans like that!" The writer, stuck in Stage One, is holding things up. In the second stage, one knows one will do evil in the world. The trick is to do smaller evils so that bigger evil will be thwarted or smashed. One gets one's nose dirty. In fact, one is part of government, and one learns to be patient with government. One practises inventing government, in fact.

Third Stage: We naturally move from Stage Two to this final one: it happens when we are exhausted from trying to change bureaucracy to responsible, merciful organizations or exhausted from trying to make altruism a larger part of our own and others' motivation. We are tired: we want to fall back into our private lives. Exhaustion is not the only force that draws us into Stage Three, however; another is a moment that comes sooner or later to everyone, even to those who are not virtuously tired. It is the moment when you perceive your death to be closer to you than your birth. It happens some blossoming afternoon when others are napping — and once it has come it never goes. Even if in the next second we shout hoarsely, "Who wants to squeeze in a fast set?" the moment is still there. Even the joyous greed, when one has whacked a net shot right past the ear of one's opponent, is tempered by the remembering: "O yes — my death had a word with me earlier today."

The moment one has met one's death a new desire is born. It is the desire to replace all conflict and whatever ethical anxiety we have borne with *physical comfort* and *psychological distractions*. People guiltless of the Kübler-Ross "Denial" syndrome until then now become classic cases. Which of us doesn't know a dozen middle- or very-aged people who haven't rather unpleasantly cut off our conversations with, "O yes, but it all works out in the end, you know!" and "Well — first and last you have to see that it's a grand old universe!" or "We have to look on the bright side of things!" They may as well have said, "What poor Salvadorans? I don't see any." Or "Well, there's no point in worrying. Jesus said we'd always have the poor with us, so we got them." An ethical person who finds himself or herself in Stage Three has to spend the rest of life juggling the temptation of pain-avoidance with the determination not to be slothful. I never sneer at noblesse oblige any more, because noblesse oblige represents the old ethical-fighter's willingness to pitch in, still, for the common weal. If that person weren't exercising noblesse oblige, he or she would be sleeping it off in Tucson or Palm Desert.

Alas, the ex-fairy tale readers slip easily into Stage Three, sometimes without having done any work in Stage Two. Noblesse oblige is not very different from what the peasant boy did who made it to the castle: that showering of gold on those using ox-carts seemed fine to us when we were introverted little kids. Now, again, it seems nice. We become our own role model of the castle dowager.

Having had a look at all three stages, let's go back to Stage One where writers often get stuck. Their simple view is that the outer world is coarse, and they do their business with it by day without trying to change it. A fairy-tale reader is someone with a taste for beautiful ideas and beautiful language. A castle is beautiful as a Project is not. Faithfulness, love, fealty, and realm are the words—not Square One, cool, with it, and pit city. When you are ten years old your hair stands on end to think of Faithful John. You wrap those lovely phrases and ideas around your soul and keep warm in there. Since you are only ten, no one has said, Now you must take those fairy-tale ideas and practise them in the marketplace. Your habit, therefore, is to love beauty and not try to translate it into merciful acts. It is the beginning of a non-political and non-ethical lifestyle. There are a thousand other childhood styles that lead to a non-political and non-ethical outlook, but their existence doesn't lessen the force of this one.

When the fairy-tale reader closes the book and slams the storm door and looks for someone to shoot baskets with, he or she finds other children who have not been reading. These children have learnt cynicism in the Saturday morning cartoons. The plot of most children's TV is put-down and mild sneering. The souls, therefore, of those who watch, don't expect nourishment. Unless there have been intense conversations with parents or there is an extraordinary storytelling grandparent in the house, the souls of such children simply wait. TV doesn't feed them. The Bears and the Patriots don't feed them. The soul doesn't feel expressed, as fairy-tale readers' souls do. There is a huge difference between a child who has made a mental image of George gashing the dragon's belly—an image of justice—and the child who has never made that mental image or any other like it. The difference in their cognitive development shows by the time they are in third grade. The reader can make mental images and transfer remembered incidents and scenes to the present to help evaluate the present circumstance. The usual finding is that the mental-image maker is capable of empathy and, therefore, it follows, of sympathy and merciful action to go with it. The non-reader can't imagine himself or herself in any sufferer's boots. The sufferer's cries don't make much sense to him or her and therefore are seen as unattractive.

Before we congratulate the fairy-tale reader, we need to look at something else: The fairy-tale reading child may have a taste for mental-image-making all right, but he or she also has a taste for simply being literary. Moral-development people pay attention to that taste for simply being literary. It is a kind of immunity to suffering.

When we tell a literary person about social changes that are needed, we see that he or she is very interested. It is enraging to find someone courteously interested and nothing more, when you are describing a specific cut in federal budgeting.

Since Reagan got in, there is so little money for disturbed, adjudicated children that this is what happens: Foster home care costs a county in Minnesota between sixteen and twenty-two dollars a day. Care at a psychiatric treatment center runs from between seventy-five to three hundred dollars a day. Because there isn't enough money for all the seriously disturbed children to receive treatment, social workers are forced to refer disturbed children to foster parents. The foster parents are not therapists, and it doesn't work. The children don't get well. The children again show up in court, and the process repeats itself. Just in case that isn't clear, here is the other half of it: Since the disturbed children are taking places in the foster homes, not all children who should be in foster homes are going there. Some children who are abused by their parents are being returned to their homes. Their social workers are agonized.

If we use social-science jargon to describe such a situation, we see a look of pain cross our hearers' faces. It is the jargon, of course. Literary people feel superior and offended by our "let's get some feedback and then develop a timeline! We're looking at ten weeks' work anyway! It'll be a year down the pike before you can implement that!" and so on. We must realize that *a taste for aesthetic language is a major psychological fact*: when people have it, it is one of their passions.

Let us say a person can feel just so many passions at any one time. If a third of our personality feels passionately about beauty, then we won't be completely happy working with tired, ungrammatical people—even though those people are putting together a strong lobby that the rest of our personality loves. If the lobbyist soul is fed by desperately trying to right wrongs, the aesthete's isn't—not completely. The aesthete longs for beautiful language which spares its readers nouns like "feedback." The psyche of such a literate person tends to separate the organizing instincts from the spiritual instincts: a literate person tends to be practical by day, resigned to the world's organizations, never mind the outcomes. Spiritual instincts get expressed in leisure activities.

In case that seems like a precious observation, let's make this hypothesis: most graduates of Andover and Yale with a college major in the humanities are basically pragmatic about the organizations they work with by day, and are interested, courteous, and literate in their conversations in the evening. After all, this is a workable adaptation to American life. Why should anyone drop it?

5

Let's follow the Andover/Yale graduate past the fairy-tale reading stage. His or her habit will be to read literature for two purposes: For enjoyment of eternal verities and for general interest.

Neither one of those two aims has anything to do with uneducated life. It is a definition of uneducated and uneducable people that they do not take an interest in what is not germane to their lives, nor in abstract concepts. That is why project directors, when drumming up local resource people, are careful to start "where the people are." Eternal verities—concepts which apply to human beings and plants and stars at different times and places—are the cultivated taste of people who can do formal operations in cognition.

Most readers of Shakespeare, for example, love him not for what we can learn about meshing economic classes in *Cori-*

olanus, or for the process of self-recognition Lear had to stop ducking, but for the soliloquies—the eternal verities: Life falls into seven stages. Ah yes, so it does. It is scary to die because if there's a life after death, like dreaming after falling asleep, and going to heaven or hell, it might be like bad dreams. Ah yes, so it might. If you are true to yourself, it follows that you won't be false to any other man. Ah yes, that does follow. To be able to point to your child and say that although your own blood is old you feel young for having had a child—ah yes, one does. The humanities student rejoices in truths that stay put.

Major flux is likely one of the least pleasant psychological experiences anyone has, well-read or poorly-read. Therapists are quick to tell us that fear of change, whether within oneself or in one's outer circumstances, is very painful. It is considerably less painful to read Shakespeare's work as eternal verity than to recognize it as a guide to social changemaking.

The eternal verity lover has a stake in novels and short stories being about love, career, private life, love of nature, and a gallant approach to death. He or she starts using the expression "universal values" in school or college and continues to use it all through life.

Tremendous shame over various acts of the United States is not yet a universal value or an eternal verity; one doesn't feel peaceable and wise reading about our dropping Atom bombs on Japan. One can't say, "Ah yes, the dropping of bombs by my country on Japan, the very day I was finishing the Summer Reading List." It is not yet an eternal verity to hear that young mothers are nervous about their breastmilk because it might carry Iodine 131 or Strontium 90 in it to the baby. Tolstoy's eternal verities about young mothers being nervous about nursing are one thing—who wants escape reading about Strontium 90 anyhow?

6

Most highly placed business and government leaders do not yet read the ethicists' books. They are still ignorant of *process* in ethics; they tend simply not to know about ethical stage development. People appear to them as one kind of person or another kind of person, as if their characters were rather fixed, in the nineteenth century perception of "character." Their novel reading is about private lives. Their "thinking" reading tends to be Naisbitt and Seymour Hersh, and everyone is conversant about Management By Walking Around from *In Search of Excellence*.

It is important to realize that moralists, as such, are invariably read in college by people who *will* become leaders, but are seldom read after that: college boys and girls read Hannah Arendt; fifty- and sixty-year-old national leaders tend not to know her work. Lawrence Kohlberg's work in stage development of moral awareness has been out for decades: his major thesis, *The Philosophy of Moral Development: Moral Stages and the Idea of Justice* was published in 1981, but the trade department at Harper & Row, who published Kohlberg, regarded it at the time as "something the College Department did." In other words, Harper & Row apparently did not assume this was a book widely and wonderfully to affect American upper-middle-class life. No one in large publishing today is a fool: the Harper & Row people were probably accurate in assuming that the trade-books reading public still wants to stay in its private life.

The second habit of the graduate fairy-tale reader is reading for amiable, general interest. I am continually astounded at the equable interest which educated people take in this or that circumstance. Reading simply for interest is conditioned in our society at every level. People who don't read much use the word "interesting" without cease. "I didn't find it very interesting," they say. "Thank you for the book of poetry. It was very interesting." Naturally, to a cross-hearted moralist that *interest* is anathema. In a burst of paranoia I find myself imagining telling someone about St. Stephen being stoned. I explain that the man later known as St. Paul held someone's coat for him so he could use both arms to stone Stephen more handily. When I finish telling it, the hearer says, "That's very interesting." Or worse: "You made it so interesting," as though everything were a question of technical prowess, not content. Educated people can be as ethically numb as non-readers. They read through pages and pages of John McPhee on oranges. Oranges! McPhee's chapter on oranges is one of the most thoroughgoing researches into a subject I've ever seen. Why would one read it?

One would read about a subject that doesn't affect one in any emotional or ethical way because of interest in *other*. We are a curious species. Of all the animals, we are the one that systematically investigates everything we can see and touch and much that we can't: we record how everything behaves and then we predict. It is great fun. It is democratic as well. One can be quite stupid and still enthusiastically learn about and take an interest in odd performances or strange data.

If we connect this odd, technical curiosity to our instinct to avoid pain, we can see that accumulating fairly meaningless information works as a pastime. A German who is an expert on butterflies, and has found a new species on the eve of September 1, 1939, is much more content than a moralist was that night. Middle-aged college-educated women support the detective story market — not in order to acquire expertise in murder or detection, but because of *interest*.

Minnesota readers, I have noticed, regularly read through Patricia Hampl's *A Romantic Education* for all the interesting material about a Saint Paulite with a Czech-American background. They are interested in the lovely, surprising details about Saint Paul, in the lovely, surprising details about the bridges of Prague, in lovely, surprising details as if they were a raison d'être for the book itself. They nearly uniformly have ignored the author's discussion of what psychological effect it has on people to live under a brutal totalitarian government — exactly how it damps thought and ardor.

We regard Hampl's seeing a connection between aesthetic and ethical experience as a forgivable quirk. Fortunately, we say, her style is strong enough to support the quirk. That's what people thought of Virginia Woolf, too. They read her for her marvelous style. They did what they could to stave off thinking about her real offering which simply was this: if you present in literature the gross suffering of one, imaginable individual person, you can make people hate and oppose a widespread cruelty. How carelessly Woolf was read! Then, fifty years later, how carelessly those in her wake are being read!

We don't mean to be heartless or stupid readers: it is just that we were told it is all right simply to be interested. We read about Andrea Lea's Radcliffe characters getting along with her Harvard characters (in *The New Yorker*). We read how Susan Champion's characters fight heartbreak by scraping dead animals off the road for the New Jersey Highway Department (*Sing Heavenly Muse!*). I don't clean New Jersey highways and never will, so I feel oddly and pleasantly *instructed* as I read Champion.

The trouble with it is that this otherness I am after is a shallow imitation of the serious otherness I would feel if I were reading empathetically. Since I prefer to feel virtuous than to feel remiss, I am likely to let myself feel virtuous when taking an interest in other people's technical circumstances. Any knitter who patiently hears out a crocheter feels virtuous; a small-grains farmer who hears out a hog-operation farmer feels virtuous. That virtue is a sop to the ethical part of us that *ought* to hear out a starving person, ask questions, collect data, stir up a group to work with, and change a policy, so the person will stop starving. As does a light-weight general interest, such empathy starts with mental-image-making. The one is pleasant, however, and the other painful.

A final remark about why our characters feel no ethical anxiety: writers, ex-fairy-tale readers as we are, literature-loving as we are, curiosity-seekers as we are, conservative lovers of static truths as we are, are further cursed by what psychologists call the Bystander Effect.

> *The [Bystander] Effect occurs, the studies show, because witnesses diffuse responsibility ["Only one person needs to call the police, and certainly someone else will"], and because they look at the behavior of the other bystanders to determine what is happening ["If no one else is helping, does this person really need help?"]. As a result, membership in a group of bystanders lowers each person's likelihood of intervening.*
>
> R. Lance Shotland, "When Bystanders Just Stand By," *Psychology Today*, June, 1985.

Our friends aren't writing novels about how nice Andover and Yale graduates love literature but govern unkindly, so we don't write the book either.

A prominent result of the Bystander Effect among writers is that we have almost no one trying to figure out why American upper-middle-class English majors grow up to be forty- and fifty- and sixty-year-old perpetrators of appalling foreign and domestic policy. Tolstoy managed to include that kind of subject in fiction without spoiling *Anna Karenina* or *The Death of Ivan Ilyitch*. Surely we can produce these elegant but wrong people in *our* stories: it would mean avoiding facile sociological barbs.

Most students of writing will not even take upper-middle-class Americans as protagonists for serious stories. I have assigned exercises in which students are asked to write for ten minutes about a photograph that shows a Dartmouth tailgating party. Invariably the students jump into a sociological categorizing of the people shown: they settle for writing quickly with apparent dislike of the rich boys and girls in the picture. If my students genuinely resent these people, then they need to stop merely griping and sneering (Griping is the impotent behavior of corporals and sergeants who have no hope of changing the army).

If we did serious, ethical studies of the middle-aged ex-preppies in our present-day Administration, wonderful pressure would be felt by the twenty-one-year-old preppy who read our stories: he or she would say inwardly, "I am seen! They understand me. What I do, ethically, apparently matters!" Such a reader would not unconsciously wander into the Reagan Administration.

7

Let us ask ourselves two questions: is our nation brutal? And can we write stories about characters who care whether or not their nation is brutal? If both answers are yes, all we have to do is create a pleasant fellow who reads Grimm, Asbjørnsen and Moe, Conrad, John Knowles, William Golding, goes to Andover or Groton and on to Swarthmore (Yes! Swarthmore! Where he should hear of the Friends' alternative notions of government abroad and at home) — and yet who amazingly, mysteriously, takes a job with a corporation that has done this, let us say: it was caught out selling harmful products here so it has withdrawn them and is selling them in the Third World instead.

Here is another outcome. He doesn't take the job with that company. He is the one of the CIA people who remembers all the elevator operators' names in his building and does not forget to stroke the German Shepherd at dusk and takes his wife and children not snowmobiling but cross-country skiing — and works ten hours a day designing American behavior in Central America.

It shouldn't be hard to make a fiction about him. We

have our journals to mine. If we have written down somewhere that *we* like to escape the family on late Christmas afternoon, to survey the silent, impersonal forest and lake, then we can give that secret Christmas practice to the CIA or Reagan Administration man. Ethical consciousness means we must be truthful: we must confess that not just New Wave types, but also CIA operatives, like to make home-gathered berries into chutney. We will need hundreds of carefully, affectionately observed details about people who make our country do what it does. We may not start out affectionately, but we will soon like these makers-of-brutality better, because we will have named things about them we never thought of before.

After all, leaders are usually very attractive. A priest in the Church of England told me impatiently, "Can't you understand that the devil *always* wears the right school tie, and that he's the one in the room with the pleasant manners?" Let us put two of these well-dressed people with ties and courtesy into a room, then. It is a large reception hall; young boys of another kind of background are passing trays of champagne. Our two men are talking to a nice woman. They are talking about oranges, because the older man and the forty-three-year-old woman have been reading McPhee on oranges. (The younger man has just finished *A Separate Peace* and *Lord of the Flies*: he mentioned them and the older two both smiled and said, "Darn good books, those — with wonderful surprising details, too!") All three like each other.

What is the literature we need to write so that the twenty-year-old will not give in to *moral drift*? If I were at the reception, I should want to come up and break into the conversation: "You are all so attractive and competent in life!" I would cry. "Don't settle for American policy as it is! Do something better! We want peace — peace! Not just leverage against the Soviet Union!"

For about one minute, rudeness itself, especially when it arrives unexpectedly at a pleasant reception, is interesting. Someone might also take in the content of the rude person's cries for justice, for about a minute, but then the years of courtesy and conventional behaviors and the ambiance of the reception hall itself will fold back over the minute's rude cry as a fog naturally enfolds a steeple. Rude remarks don't seem *real* to people used to intelligent conventions: they scorn the rudeness and stop hearing.

However intelligent our conventions, they are forces of *moral drift*. Ethical thinkers call it moral drift when we start out feeling strongly about something, but — since we are courteous — we listen to all our colleagues' ideas on that same subject; they are a little averse to our opinion, so we modify our stance. We may even do an about-face. Anyone who has done jury duty will recognize moral drift; liberal groups who believe in consensus unconsciously force their dissenting members into moral drift — lest no one get home that night.

Let's go back to the young man in his good tie, with his conventional good school just behind him, with his future as a colleague of the uncle he is listening to or of other men like his uncle. His mother stands there, looking very moved by something, and now and again glancing at him. Not ten years behind him is all his reading of fairy-tale adventures, where the hero is a lone young person who makes it in the wide world. He knows that the modern-day phrase for "and governed the people wisely and well to the end of his days" is "and joined the State Department where he worked diligently to protect his country's safety from all the rest of the world." The uncle is now singing *sotto voce* with his mother, laughing a little as they sing, so standers-by and the host will see they are having a quiet, workable, musical joke, not a drunken singsong. His job is arranging violence against hold-out peasants in Central America.

What is the literature we should write for the young man? As Hamlet did, we need a play. We don't need the play to catch the conscience of the uncle so much as to stop moral drift in the nephew. It should honor the disgust and fear the young man already half-feels for what his uncle does. We must *name* that disgust and fear.

Thousands of American kids learned to laugh irreverently at phonies because they had read Salinger's great scene in which Holden Caulfield tells us that Pencey Prep's history teacher may pretend not to be picking his nose but he is picking it, just the same. Salinger's great gift to psychologically unconscious, highly educated people was showing how different motives appear and motives are.

Salinger brought psychological wakening to the privileged. We want to bring in *ethical* wakening. All we have to do is look harder at the scene we have already imagined. We will have an interior dialogue, let's say, because that is the easiest way to move from one's own feeling into the feeling of a story character. We must make a guess about what the young man is feeling about his uncle. Here is a rough go:

> The guy's incredible: I love him! I love him! He looks like a bear with that slouch, too. A bear with a Countess Mara tie on and he hangs onto the gingerale as if it were a whisky. And he loves Aunt Bev OK and he likes the whole family; here are he and Mom acting like kids again, but you know, even when he is gassing around with Mom there is something puke-making about Uncle Jim. Like now he has praised Mom for her gooseberry conserve about eight times and told her how he serves Aunt Bev breakfast on weekends, and the kids when they're home from anywhere, and Aunt Bev was knocked out by the gooseberry conserve, too. On the other hand I should shut up once, why don't I. Mom looks happy. She looks happy and heartbroken at the same time, the way all old women in their forties do; they lose the clean look of one thing or the other somehow. O God now she is asking him to do the last verse of that song again. O God they're both doing it. "In after years should troubles arise/To cloud the blue of sunny skies . . . " O God keep it down please, guys (someone pauses to greet the nephew). Hello, Mr. Weinberger, good to see *you*, sir (someone else comes past with a tray of stemmed glasses) Hi, yeah, thanks, I'll take another . . . I wonder what it's like to be a busboy all your life, keep it down, uncle and mother. You'd never know Uncle Jim gets all that glitz bucks to help contras hurt people. It's amazing. Makes me edgy. On the other hand, he is not faking it about liking to sing that song and when he gets done with that one, knowing him, he will help Mom sing one of hers and he'll know the words, too, O God Jesus they are pulling their handkerchiefs out for the finale. O well, it isn't that Uncle Jim ever *denies* exactly what he does down there with all those contras. He just forgets, I guess. Anyway, this isn't a confessional or the War Room. It's a party, for God's sake.

Why does the young man protest to God so many times? What does he see? He sees that his uncle is exorbitant in his attention to domestic affairs (as is our literature). The uncle is being very pleasant about light-weight things (as is too much of our literature). The uncle is not looking at the huge evil he himself does. Our literature has not yet agreed to look at it, either.